Marty Mouse Goes Somewhere

Written by David Adlington

Illustrated by Chad Parker

MartyMouseGoesSomewhere.com

ISBN 979-8-90148-095-3

THIS BOOK BELONGS TO: _____

Marty Mouse Goes Somewhere
Second Edition – 2025
(First Published in 1993)
Copyright © 1993–2025 **David Adlington**
Illustrations Copyright © 1993–2025 **Chad Parker**

This book is a revised second edition of Marty Mouse Goes Somewhere, originally published in 1993.
Printed in the United States of America

ISBN: ISBN 979-8-90148-095-3

Re-publisher in Partnership with Truth Communications Media & Publications
www.TruthCommunications.org

Copies of Marty Mouse Goes Somewhere are available from
MartyMouseGoesSomewhere.com
Special rates are available to non-profit groups who wish to use
this book as a fundraising venture.

Dedication
Marty Mouse Goes Somewhere
(Second Edition)

It has been quite a journey since Marty Mouse Goes Somewhere was first written in the fall of 1981, published in 1993, and now revised for this second edition in 2025.

Many of the people once mentioned have since passed on, including my parents (Ray and Vera Adlington) and their generation, all of whom have left a lasting impression on my life. I dedicate this edition to their memory and to the influence they will continue to have.

To the children who once delighted in Marty's adventure, now grown and some with children of their own, I hope that Marty and his friends will continue to bring joy for many years to come.

To those meeting Marty and his friends now, I hope that you will enjoy reading this book and the others to follow. Thanks to Wayne Hinds and the staff at Truth Communications for preparing this second edition.

David Adlington
Trinity, North Carolina, USA
December 2025

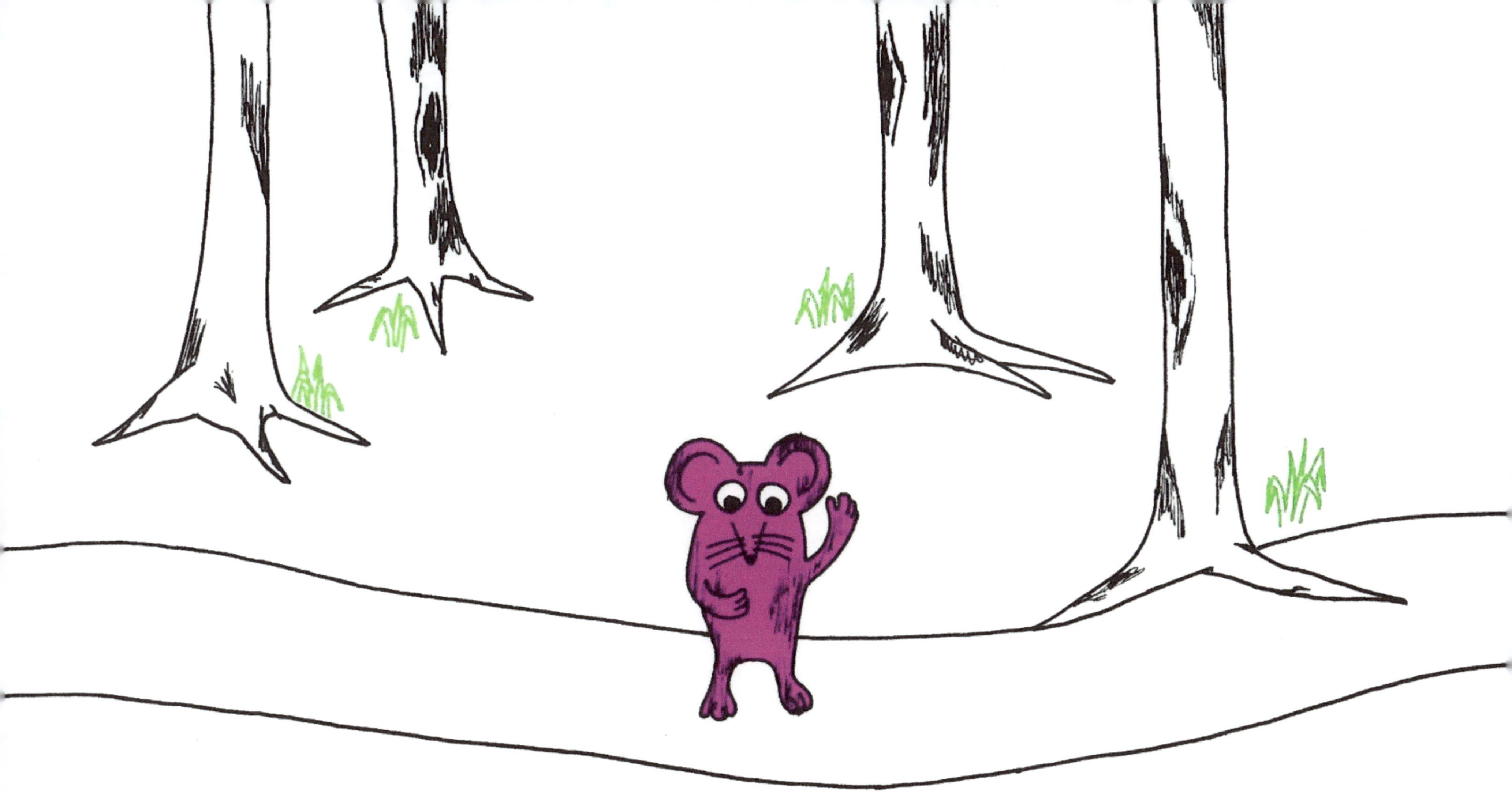

This is **Marty Mouse** waving "Hello."
Marty Mouse lives in the woods.

One day **Marty Mouse** started walking through the woods.

He was going somewhere.

Marty Mouse walked by Bobbi Bird.

Bobbi Bird decided to follow **Marty Mouse** to see where he was going.

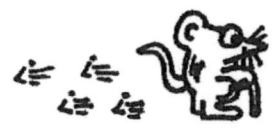

Marty Mouse and Bobbi Bird
walked by Sandra Squirrel.

Sandra Squirrel decided to follow
Bobbi Bird to see where **Marty
Mouse** was going.

Marty Mouse, Bobbi Bird, and Sandra
Squirrel walked by Billy Beaver.

Billy Beaver decided to follow Sandra Squirrel and Bobbi Bird to see where **Marty Mouse** was going.

Marty Mouse, Bobbi Bird, Sandra Squirrel, and Billy Beaver walked by Ryan Rabbit.

Ryan Rabbit decided to follow Billy Beaver, Sandra Squirrel, and Bobbi Bird to see where **Marty Mouse** was going.

Marty Mouse, Bobbi Bird, Sandra Squirrel, Billy Beaver, and Ryan Rabbit walked by Orest Owl.

Orest Owl decided to follow Ryan
Rabbit, Billy Beaver, Sandra Squirrel,
and Bobbi Bird to see where **Marty
Mouse** was going.

Marty Mouse, Bobbi Bird, Sandra Squirrel, Billy Beaver, Ryan Rabbit, and Orest Owl walked by Little Lake.

Marty Mouse stopped. Bobbi Bird stopped.
Sandra Squirrel stopped. Billy Beaver stopped.
Ryan Rabbit stopped.

Orest Owl stopped. Where do you think **Marty Mouse** was going?

To Little Lake of course. He was thirsty.

Educational Activities

Discuss the following questions with your child.

Language Arts

1. Do you remember the name of the squirrel? What is it?

2. What is the name of the rabbit?

3. What kind of animal is Marty?

4. What do you do when you are thirsty?

5. What do you think Marty Mouse found at Little Lake?

6. Why did the other animals go to Little Lake?

7. Tell the story and add more animals walking to the Lake.

8. What might the animals do for fun at Little Lake?

9. What do you think the friends might be saying to one another as they are having fun at Little Lake?

10. Act out parts of the story and/or make puppets.

Mathematics

1. Using the pages in the book as a guide, count from 1 - 20.

2. On lined paper trace some numbers.

3. Describe what you see on page 8 and 9.

4. On what page does the story end?

5. Can you say these numbers: 1   3   6   7   9   10   13   20

Character Colors: Marty & Friends

Bring Marty Mouse and his friends to life with your crayons or colored pencils.
You can use the colors shown below for each character.

Orest Owl	Ryan Rabbit	Billy Beaver	Sandra Squirrel	Bobbi Bird	Marty Mouse
Black	Green	Red	Orange	Yellow	Purple

www.ingramcontent.com/pod-product-compliance
Lightning Source LLC
Chambersburg PA
CBHW040819120626
46551CB00004B/604